AMAZON

FIRE TV

Author: John Slavio

TABLE OF CONTENTS

DISCLAIMER

ABOUT THE AUTHOR

John Slavio is a programmer who is passionate about the reach of the internet and the interaction of the internet with daily devices. He has automated several home devices to make them 'smart' and connect them to high speed internet. His passions involve computer security, iOT, hardware programming and blogging.

INTRODUCTION

Amazon Fire TV is way to stream different media types from the Internet onto your TV. This means that you can watch videos or listen to music from the internet, even if you don't have cable. Live sports games can be streamed onto your TV. This is a big advantage for those who do not want to buy cable or satellite or those who are trying to cut costs out of their budget. You will merely need to pay the original cost of the Amazon Fire TV box, but you will be able to avoid paying regular, monthly costs. Channels and apps commonly streamed include Netflix, Hulu, Amazon Video, HGTV, FOX, and ESPN. However, Amazon Fire TV contains one of the largest selections of streaming options, and you will find many more channels available than the few listed here.

In this introduction, you will learn answers to a few key questions to may have as you are considering purchasing an Amazon Fire TV. The questions answered are: what is Amazon Fire TV, what are the differences between the Fire Stick and the Fire TV, and why purchase an Amazon Fire TV?

What is Amazon Fire TV?

Like described above, Amazon Fire TV is a streaming device. However, you should know a little bit more about it than that. Firstly, this device has 2GB of memory, so you will have plenty of space to save your favorite movies. Additionally, this space can be expanded using a USB and connecting it to one of the Amazon Fire TV's ports. This device also works at a higher speed than the first model which was released in April of 2014.

Additionally, the new model has 4K Ultra High Definition support. Most of its features work through Bluetooth, meaning that you can connect to the box using your kindle or computer. This also means that you can connect to the box using headphones so that you can watch a movie or play a game without the whole house needing to hear it. Instructions on how to make these connections will be explained more fully later in this guide.

Basically, the Amazon Fire TV is a way to stream the internet onto your TV in a fast and easy-to-understand way. This product was designed in such a way that even those who have trouble understanding technology will be able to easily navigate this system.

What are the Differences Between the Fire TV Stick and Fire TV?

Another Amazon product that has also become popular is the Fire TV Stick. This book is specifically about Amazon Fire TV, not the stick; however, it will help you be an informed buyer if you know the differences and if buying a Fire TV Stick in addition to your Amazon Fire TV will be beneficial or not.

Firstly, the Fire TV Stick is a much smaller device. However, that also means that the stick has half the memory. Games that require a lot of space, for example Minecraft, would not work well with the stick. You would need the box and perhaps an extra memory card to run high-functioning games well. It does come with 8GB of storage in addition to 1GB of memory, but that will go quickly.

The stick is very limited in ways that you can connect with it. One side has a USB port and the other one has a HDM1 port. However, it does have Bluetooth capabilities, and you can connect with it via your Amazon account online.

However, the Amazon Fire TV box has these components and more. You can expand the box's memory with its memory slot, and you will have access to the digital audio port or Ethernet port. The two devices are different in the way they display images. Check with your TV to see which device will display a clearer picture. In some cases, the images will be very similar.

Last of all, one of the most obvious differences in the two devices is the price. The stick costs around $50 less than the box. However, you must weigh in its limited features to see if saving the money will still give you all the features you want. The best way to explain the differences is to say that the Fire Stick is a more compact version of the Amazon Fire TV.

Why Purchase an Amazon Fire?

With so many gaming devices now available that can stream movies or Netflix, you may wonder what this device can do that a simple Wii, for example, cannot. Many people may ask why they need another device when they already have so many devices plugged up to their TV. There are three simple reasons why the Amazon Fire TV would be a good choice for your internet streaming needs. As we dive into how to work with the Amazon Fire TV, you will see exactly how true these are.

- Easy- This device is easy to use. While some of its more advanced features may require some studying to work, the basic functions of the device are easily understandable. Once you have set up the box (the process is thoroughly explained in the first chapter), a tutorial will play, walking you through its basic features and setting you up for immediate use.

- Fast- Some devices become bogged down when they have a lot in their memory. You end up waiting a long time to watch your programs. However, the Amazon Fire TV box will not keep you waiting for long. If its memory is filled, it has a Cloud that can store movies, etc. All you need is internet to connect to the Cloud. Also, the speed Amazon Fire TV takes to pull up a movie is incredibly fast.
- Multiple features- Some prospective buyers do not know that the Amazon Fire TV box can double as a gaming device. You can stream internet games and use your controllers to play them on your TV.

In the upcoming chapters, you will learn what makes this internet streaming device unique from other similar devices. You will learn how to set up and begin using the Amazon Fire TV box. Last of all, you will also learn the basic commands for this box, including using voice commands for playing and watching on your Amazon Fire TV box.

COMPARING AMAZON FIRE TO CHROMECAST, APPLE TV, AND ROKU

Amazon came out with their Fire TV a bit after than some of the other companies started producing their streaming devices. What does this mean? This means that Amazon got the opportunity to see how the other devices worked and what people disliked about them. Then, they could incorporate that information into the formation of their own product, meaning that the Fire TV product has a few features that make it stand out. Let's look at the major benefit for each of the following devices: Amazon Fire TV, Chromecast, Apple TV, and Roku.

Amazon Fire TV: Amazon Fire TV offers the unique option of a remote. It also offers a smaller version, the Fire TV Stick referenced earlier. One more unique benefit Amazon Fire TV offers is security when you use your pin number to buy things. This is helpful in case you have guests over or sneaky children. The updated version of the Amazon Fire TV has a few extra benefits, because Amazon heard the complaints of their users and changed their system to better serve them.

Chromecast: Chromecast is a very low-cost option that sells between $30 and $35. Also, it streams a very wide variety of shows.

Apple TV: This device is for those who already have a big ITunes profile. Why? Apple TV can stream ITunes music, with which many other devices will not have access. This is the main benefit, but if you do not have ITunes, then this device does not really have an outstanding benefit for you.

Roku: There are several different versions of Roku on the market. Roku 2, 3, and 4 all have different advantages and different costs. These costs range from around $50 up to $130 or so. The Roku 2 can connect to an Ethernet box, solving any problems you have with Wi-fi. The most expensive Roku device also streams 4k shows.

What About Negative Factors?

There are always parts of a device that could have been manufactured better or changed just a bit to add some extra features. No device is perfect. So, you want to know exactly what the problem is with each device so that you know what you are getting into. Let's look at them.

Amazon Fire TV: The main disadvantage of this device is that it is one of the pricier options, even compared to its own Fire Stick. However, if you are receiving more features for the price, then the purchase could be worth the money it costs.

17

Chromecast: Chromecast does not come with a remote. You must use your phone or tablet to control this device, which can be problematic. Most of all, it means that you must have another device capable of streaming at high speed. For example, if your phone is slow, then there is only so much the streaming speed you can get.

Apple TV: As with Chromecast, one of its benefits can also be its downfall. Because Apple TV is the only device that has access to your ITunes songs, you must select this one to listen to your songs. However, if you do not have an ITunes account, then this device does not offer anything that helps it stand out.

Roku: The biggest disadvantage for this device is also its hefty price tag. If you want to get 4k streaming, then you will need to pay a higher amount. If you already have a lot of devices around your TV or have already invested a lot of money in a gaming system, investing more than $100 in another device may not be worth it.

Time to Make a Choice:

So, now it comes time to make your choice. If you have already bought an Amazon Fire TV box, then you have already made your choice. If not, I recommend buying it. Why? This device is the only device that has access to Amazon TV and videos. Amazon Prime offers unlimited streaming, so choosing to have a device that connects with your account means that you will have unlimited streaming on your TV. While pretty much all streaming devices can connect to Netflix or YouTube, Amazon's Fire TV will give you extra access along with access to Netflix, YouTube, and others.

With other devices, you may be able to connect to Amazon streaming, but the apps do not come on the devices. You must use a casting device to stream

Amazon video. If your main way of watching TV is through Amazon, having a device that was created to stream that video will be most beneficial to you. Additionally, with an Amazon Fire TV, you can order Amazon products using the box or even the voice controller. This can be beneficial if you are listening to a song you like, and you want to buy it right away. You may also be cooking while you are watching TV. You can use the voice commands to add an ingredient to your shopping list.

Last of all, Amazon Fire TV has the most well-built, powerful hardware. It is very user friendly, and the extra price is worth it for the features and easy access to Amazon video streaming. Check out the next chapter for a full explanation on set up and installation.

SET UP AND INSTALLATION OF AMAZON FIRE TV

Setting up your Amazon Fire TV box correctly is an important step, and you should carefully follow these directions so that you will be able to set up the device without having any problems. The time it takes to read the instructions are worth it as you may be able to control features you did not even know were available if you had not read the instructions.

Required Equipment:

These are the items that will come in your Amazon Fire TV box.

- Amazon Fire Device- This is the black box.

- Voice Remote- This looks like a regular remote, except with relatively few buttons.
- Power Connection- This is a cord that connects the device to your power source.
- Two AAA Batteries- These will be used for the remote.

These are the items you will need that you must buy separately.

- Internet Connection- Obviously, if you will be streaming shows from the internet, you will need an internet connection. Specifically, HD streaming, even if it has a low broadband speed, will give you positive results. You should generally have a connection that has a minimum of 1.5 mbps or you will find yourself frustrated with the speed. If your internet works quickly, the box will also.

- Television- The Amazon Fire TV box needs to connect with an HDM1 connection port on your TV. If your TV does not have one of these, then you need to look for a converter- something that will connect to the port your TV has and provide an HDM1 connection for your Amazon Fire TV as well.

- HDM1 Cable- You will need a cable to connect the Amazon Fire TV to your television, and this cable is NOT INCLUDED. You can find one for a low cost, but you need to have it ready when it is time to install the Fire TV or you will not be able to use it immediately.

- Amazon Account- Last of all, you will need an Amazon account. Creating an

Amazon account is free and easy. If you
wish to have an Amazon Prime account,
you will have access to many more
videos. HINT: If you are a student and
have a student email, you can access
Amazon Prime for free while you are in
school. This account provides free
shipping, music, and videos, which is an
excellent perk.

Properly Set Up Hardware:

Now that you have the materials you will need;
you must put the pieces together. These steps are simple
and have been written so that novel users can
understand.

1. Using the HDM1 cable, you should
   connect the device to the port on your

TV. If your TV has multiple ports, the port number that you connect it with will be the channel you will need to access the box (HDM1 port = HDM1 channel, HDM2 port = HDM2 channel, etc).

2. Connect the Amazon Fire TV box to the power source using the power cord that was included in your purchase. Turn on your Amazon Fire TV.

3. Use your television's remote to change the channel to the appropriate HDM source. This can often be done by searching for an input or video source button on your remote and selecting from the options that appear on the screen. If the Amazon Fire TV box is turned on and you have located the right channel, you should see the Fire TV logo that will let

you know you have started the box correctly.

4. Insert the included batteries into your new remote. The producers of the remote advice that it may be difficult to open the remote and extra force may be necessary. Make sure you insert both batteries positive side up.

    TROUBLESHOOTING: If your remote does not automatically connect with the box, try pressing the home icon for a minimum of five seconds, then trying pressing the play/pause button until you get a response.

5. Next, you will need to connect your device to the internet. Depending on your internet connection (wireless, wired, public), the instructions are different.

Please look below and find the
instructions that apply to your connection.

- Wired Internet Connection- If you
  are using a wired internet
  connection, you should have an
  Ethernet cable available as this is
  not included in the purchase of an
  Amazon Fire TV. Use the cable to
  connect your box to the internet
  router. Use your remote to find
  Settings, System, Network, then
  Wired. You should be able to
  select and connect.

- Wireless Internet Connection-
  Follow this series of buttons to
  connect to any available wireless
  network: **Settings, System,** then
  Wi-fi. You should see the title of
  your network and can type in your

27

network's password. If you are
having trouble locating your
internet's router using the Amazon
Fire TV box, then try shutting off
and restarting the internet router,
removing the internet router from
an enclosed space (that could
block the signal), or rescanning
for available signals.

- Public Internet Connection- You
can travel with your Amazon Fire
TV box, and connecting to public
internet signals does not need to
be difficult. This feature can be
useful if you are staying in a hotel,
renting a condo or house for a
time, etc. You will follow the
above steps for a wireless internet
connection. Once you have

selected a network, it may require you to sign in as some public networks do, and an internet page will automatically pop up so that you can sign in. By using the Menu button, you can use the remote as a pointer to click on areas that require text or a "terms and conditions" field.

6. Now, you will finish the set up by creating or entering your Amazon account. If you already have an account, then you will merely need to enter your account information. You can also create a new account or choose to have an Amazon Prime account. You will have a keyboard onscreen to help you complete the fields.

7. Entrance to your account will cause a
    tutorial to play that will explain your
    remote's functions and abilities.

Parental Controls:

Now that you have the device set up, you may want to set up a few specific features within the Amazon Fire TV. One important feature that many families may want to have are parental controls. This will allow young children to only have access to appropriate content along with not having the ability to make purchases. A feature that is part of the Amazon Fire TV is the Freetime. This Freetime is for children. They need a password to go into another account, and you, as the parent, will be the only one that has that password. One of the good things about the PIN number is that it is hidden. If you had a previously created Amazon account, you might already have the PIN for instant video access set.

To set a PIN and control settings, go to the Amazon Instant Video Settings and find the Parental Controls section. You will be able to set or reset your pin (five digits) and decide if you want restrictions on purchases. If you choose to have that setting on, someone who wants to make a purchase must know the pin number. This will keep your children from making purchases without your knowledge or accidentally.

Once you have a PIN, you can set up Freetime accounts for your children. You will select **Settings** then **Freetime and Parental Controls**. You will need to turn the parental controls on before you can select the videos that will be available to your child. There are age ranges based on TV ratings that you can select to be available for each Freetime account. From this place, you can select various devices within your Amazon account and set different controls for each one. This means that you can control each child's Kindle from your Amazon Fire TV box.

To set up and manage a child's Freetime account, you would go to **Freetime Settings** under the Parental Controls. You can set a time limit of how long the device can be used in a day. You can also select what time the device will automatically turn off. This is a great feature if you don't want your child staying up late playing games or watching shows.

The controls Amazon Fire TV offers for both itself and the devices connected with its account are excellent. It allows you as a parent to relax and be assured that your children will not be viewing anything inappropriate. Keeping your PIN number a secret and changing it often will assure that your children will be kept safe and unable to access content that would not be appropriate for them.

You are now ready to start enjoying your Amazon Fire TV box and its streaming abilities! Check out the next chapter for specific tips on how to stream video and music.

WATCHING AND LISTENING WITH AMAZON FIRE TV

You now have everything set up, and you are ready to begin enjoying your device. In the following chapters, we will talk about different methods and controls that you can use for your different media needs. In this chapter, you will learn how to stream shows and movies onto your TV, how to play music using different accounts, and how to make purchases of movies or music.

Watching TV:

Your material will be sorted based on how you obtained it. If the show or movie you want to watch is not from Amazon, you will need to access that specific app. This will follow much the same process as any gaming system that allows you access to a Netflix app for example.

If you are going to watch Amazon material, you have two options: you can watch Prime material that is streamed for free or you can watch Amazon material that you have chosen to rent or buy. To access rented or bought material, you will need to access your **Video Library** from your Home screen. From the Home screen, you can also go to **Prime Video** where you will have access to a plethora of watching options.

Stream from a Device:

If you want to connect your device to the television to watch something on your television that you might normally watch on your phone, you can use the Amazon Fire TV's Miracast feature. Before you begin trying to connect a device to your TV, you should know these tips. Firstly, your smaller device must be an

Amazon product- Fire phone or tablet (some Android model phones are also compatible)- and the device you wish to mirror must be logged into the same Amazon account. For a Kindle, your device is registered with an account. Secondly, you must also be connected to the same internet connection. Last of all, your devices must be relatively close. If they are in the same room, you shouldn't have a problem. The usual rule of thumb with this is less than twenty-five feet or so apart.

The specific steps for each device differ, but the main steps you will follow are these.

1. You need to find a button in your settings that says **Display** or **Display and Sounds**.
2. Next, you should have an option that says **Display Mirroring** or **Enable Mirracast**.

3. A list of devices will appear, and you will select your Amazon Fire TV box and wait a few moments for the screen of your handheld device to appear on the screen.

4. When you are done, you can press **Stop Mirroring** to end the connection. If you are using an Android device, you will simply move the Amazon Fire TV's remote to activate its control and stop the mirroring.

X-Ray Information:

Amazon Fire TV has X-Ray which, as its name suggests, allows you to get a little more information about something. This feature is for those who don't just like to enjoy a movie, but also like to know more about actors, music, and what is behind the movie.

X-Ray is powered by IMDb, which as you may know, is an all-inclusive listing of actors, movies, shows, and songs. Performers have their "resumes" there that connect everything. When you are watching a movie and you see a familiar face, X-Ray helps you place that face with a name, even when your memory is not serving you.

X-Ray is easy to activate. All you need to do is hit the pause button while you are watching a movie. Because you are using the Amazon Fire TV box, the names of any actors in the screen along with any music will pop up. An added feature for this is that you can select the song and immediately make a purchase, if the song is available on Amazon. This feature allows you to watch movies and get a little bit of a deeper dip into what is behind them.

One note is that this feature is only available if you are online. If you have downloaded a video to watch while offline, then you will not have access to X-Ray. However, if you are connected to internet, you are good to go.

Captioning:

Next, you may be interested in having captions. This can be a positive feature if you are hard of hearing, don't have headphones, or simply like to make sure you've understood everything. Another fun way to use closed captioning is with another language. If you are learning a language, you can choose to have the audio in the foreign language and the captions in your native language or vice versa.

Not all videos have closed captioning available, though a large amount do. A show or movie's information page will have the letters "CC" to indicate that it offers closed captioning.

Once the video or movie has started, you can select the **Menu** button and select to turn the captions on. You can select the size of the captions if you want them large or small. To turn the captions off, follow the same procedure, except now you will see that the button says **Turn Captions Off.**

Buying and Renting Shows or Movies

To select a show or movie, you will need to access it first by either searching through a category or searching for the specific name of the purchase you wish to make. You can select the video or movie and see its details. You will then be able to select whether you would like to buy or rent. Some titles may only have one option available. Once the titles are bought, they should appear in your library for your viewing.

If you would like to save a title for a later purchase, you can choose **Add to Watchlist.** If a title is new, it may be more expensive. By adding it to your watchlist, you can keep an eye on the price. This can also be a good way to keep your rented library neat and organized.

Listen to Your Music:

You can access music from your music library or from Amazon Prime if you have a Prime account. Having an Amazon Prime account means that you will have access to many albums, online and offline, that you would normally need to purchase. With music alone, the Amazon Prime account will pay for itself.

You can select music from a recently played list, or in Amazon Prime, you can look at popular songs, etc. You can make playlists and have the songs play while you are using your device for something else that does not have an audio component (such as a movie or video). By pressing the Menu button, you can return to the song you are playing.

X-Ray Strikes Again:

The same benefits that you see with X-Ray in movies also applies to music. X-Ray will display the lyrics so that you can follow along to songs you are listening to or watching. As you are browsing through your music, you should see which ones have lyrics with a clear mark on either the album, if all songs have it, or on the individual song titles.

This feature can also help you skip to certain parts of the song, go back, or go forward in the lyrics. When you are on the screen that is displaying the song lyrics, you can use the up and down buttons to scroll through the lyrics. If you want to skip to a certain section, find the section in the lyrics, then press the

Select button. This feature is only available if you own the music, not if you are streaming it.

These are the features and basic instructions for working with movies, videos, and music. You are now able to make purchases, view media that you own, and view Prime media. If you are interested in how voice searching and commands work, continue reading the next chapter.

VOICE SEARCH ON AMAZON FIRE TV (ALEXA)

One of the best features about Amazon Fire TV is that it follows voice commands. Users have said that Amazon Fire TV's Alexa is one of the best and most responsive voice command system that they have used. Amazon has put a lot of effort into making Alexa both useful and personable. To correctly use voice commands, you need to learn some of the basic commands.

Summoning Alexa

To begin giving voice commands, you need to press the microphone button on your remote. In the next chapter, you will learn about the Amazon Fire TV controller. If you have the controller, you can also press the microphone button on your controller to begin giving commands.

Basic Commands

Because Alexa first became popular with the Amazon Echo, many of the commands are the same. The different between the commands with Amazon Fire TV and Amazon Echo is that you do not need to say Alexa's name before each command ("Alexa, find the. . ."). You will simply press the microphone button and say the command. The best part of this feature is that you don't need to say the commands exactly. Alexa can understand what you are saying, even if you say it in a slightly different way. Also, her understanding improves over time.

- Volume: "Set volume to 8," or "Turn up volume" or "Mute."

- Searching Game, Music, or Video Store: "Find _____" Fill in the name of the actor, actress, song, singer, or TV show. Alexa will then search through and find titles relevant to your search.
- Request Help: "Help."

Media Commands

- Play a specific type of music: "Play pop music" or "Play music by Adele."
- Play music on an app on your Amazon Fire TV: "Play Taylor Swift station on Pandora."
- Ask information on what is playing: "What's playing?"
- Music controls: "Skip song" or "next" or "restart."
- If you are listening to Prime music and you want to add it to your list: "Add this song."

- React to music on music station apps: "Thumbs up" or "Thumbs down."
- Open Apps: "Open Netflix."

Settings:

- Set a timer: "Set a timer for three minutes."
- Set an alarm: "Set an alarm for Thursday at 5:00 am."
- Check timers: "How much time is left on timer one?'
- Cancel timer/ alarm: "Cancel alarm for Tuesday at 7:00 pm" or "Cancel eight-minute timer".

Information:

Alexa can be used to answer any basic question that you might ask through a search engine. Here are some examples of questions you can ask to receive information.

- What day is it?

- What time is it?

- What time is in France?

- What's the weather like today?

- What will the weather be on Saturday?

- What is the IMDb rating for (movie name)?

- Who plays (character's name) in (movie name)?

- Who sings (song title)?

- What was the score of the (team's name) game?

- When is (team name) next playing?

- What is forty divided by eight? (or any other basic math equation)

- How do you spell hippopotamus?

- What is a synonym for sweet?

Buying:

You can also use the voice commands to make purchases. Here are a few sample orders you might give.

- Add eggs to my shopping list.
- Buy (song) by (artist).

- Add an HDM1 cord to my cart.

Connections Outside Amazon Fire TV:

This voice command system is not reaching outside Amazon Fire TV. If you have smart home devices, you can use Alexa to command them. Common commands might be closing the garage door, changing the thermostat, or turning your lights off. Depending on the smart devices you have in your home, you may or may not be able to use this feature.

Have Some Fun!

Alexa was created not only to help you out, but also to give you some fun. You can try asking her anything, and she'll be sure to provide you with some humor. Here are a few questions and commands you might try to have some fun.

- What should I wear for Halloween?
- This statement is false.

49

- Do blondes have more fun?
- Are there UFOs?
- Random fact.
- What is the sound of one hand clapping?
- How do I get rid of a dead body?
- What is love?
- How are babies made?
- What is the loneliest number?

There are many more, but there are a few to get you started. If you are interested in seeing a more complete list, go to the last chapter in this book. That will give you a more comprehensive list of Alexa's fun commands.

GAMES AND APPS ON AMAZON FIRE TV

Besides watching and listening on the Amazon Fire TV, you can also play games and use other apps. If you have the right controllers, Amazon Fire TV can even function as a gaming system for those who are not serious gamers. Below you will find some of the basic instructions for setting up and using games and apps with Amazon Fire TV along with information on specific games that work well and game controllers that can be used.

Which Game Controller Suits the Amazon Fire TV?

There is a gaming controller that has been created specifically to be compatible with Amazon Fire TV. This game controller is sold separately and will be discussed more in detail a little further on. However, you may not need to make an extra purchase. Gaming controllers that you already have may be compatible with the Amazon Fire TV. This goes for wired and wireless gaming controllers. Let's look as some different brands and see which game controller would be a good fit for the Amazon Fire TV.

- Amazon Fire TV Controller- This controller was designed to work well with Amazon Fire TV and must be called the most compatible for that reason. This controller is connected by Bluetooth and does not need to be plugged in. It offers some features which you will not find on other controllers. Foremost, this control has a built-in microphone which allows you to control Alexa (as discussed in the previous chapter). It also provides a place for you to plug your headphones into your controller. Because this controller works best with Amazon Fire TV, it is recommended for best results.

- Xbox 360 Wired Controller- Though not the best option, this is a great follow-up option. This makes a great second option as it forgoes batteries, charging controllers, etc. You can connect the controller to your Amazon Fire TV using the USB port on the box. If you want to use the wireless version, you must have Microsoft Xbox 360 Wireless Receiver for Windows, making the wired version a simpler option. If you already have this controller in your home, you can save some money by using it.
- Dualshock 4 Bluetooth Controller- This controller is connected to Bluetooth, making the setup extremely easy. You

simply turn on your Amazon Fire TV's Bluetooth capability.

If you don't have one of the above two controllers, you may consider buying the Amazon Fire TV controller as its design allows it to be the best one for gaming with the Amazon Fire.

Using the Amazon Fire TV Controller:

Knowing the basic controls for the controller will help make your gaming experience easy. This controller is set up to take the place of the remote, so that you can play games and control your movies with one controller.

Other than the basic controls, the Amazon Fire TV controller has a few unique buttons. First, it has a button that looks like a beach ball. This beach ball is the GameCircle dashboard. It can take you to your library of games while you are in the middle of a game. Other controllers will not have this button, meaning that you will need to navigate differently.

Also, the controller has lights that will indicate the player number of the controller. This is helpful in multiplayer games where player numbers are used.

Buying and Downloading Games for Your Amazon Fire TV:

When you want to buy, or download a game for your device, you are going to follow much the same process as you followed when downloading a movie or music. You will search under the games and apps section. You should make sure that the app or game is compatible with the Amazon Fire TV. You will know that based on what is displayed in the box that says "Works With." You can then buy or download the app.

Once the app has finished downloading, you can open it and begin playing. To play a game you have downloaded, you will need to go to your game library or your apps library and find the game. You will click to open it.

I'm Tired of In-App Purchases:

Here's a hint for those of you who enjoy free games. There are often going to be advertisements and options to purchase upgrades. Because of 1-click purchasing, it can often be easy to accidentally purchase an item. Knowing how to TURN OFF in-app purchasing can save you some time and frustration.

Parental controls are your answer to saving you this trouble. Parental controls allow you to put in a PIN number that is required to make a purchase. You can no longer accidentally purchase something if you must put in the PIN number first. If you want to set up parental controls (you can select which parental controls you want to use), go back to the chapter entitled "Set Up and

Installation of Amazon Fire TV." This chapter will give you a detailed explanation of how you can set a PIN number.

Best Apps for Your Amazon Fire TV:

Sometimes, you know you'll know it when you find it, but you just don't know how to find it yet. If you are looking for some apps that will better your Amazon Fire TV experience, these apps are just what you are looking for. Some of these apps help you do things while others are games.

- VLC For Fire- This is a free app, and it helps the streaming aspect of your Amazon Fire TV. What does it do? It allows the Amazon Fire TV box to access saved files and media that you might have stored on your computer. If you saved videos from an old video camera on your computer, you can use this app to stream them onto your TV and share them with family that has come to visit.

- The Wolf Among Us- This is a game, and the first episode is free. It is an adventure game that could be compared to The Walking Dead. The basic premise of the game is that it is built around fairytale characters who are disguised as humans. You must solve the murder mystery. If you have already finished some of your favorite video games, this can be a great new adventure for the Amazon Fire TV.

- Terraria- This game costs under five dollars and is like the Minecraft's two-dimensional world. This is a multiplayer game and can be a great one for younger players.

- You Don't Know Jack Party- This game is a trivia game for the nerds in your family. It can be family friendly and is free, though in-app purchases will be offered.
- Twitch- This game allows you to watch professional, high-level players beat higher levels in games. You may have never thought that watching people play a video game can be entertaining, but it can help you learn. Users have said that it can be fun to watch players beat levels they have not even reached. Best of all, it's free.
- Daily Burn- This app has a free trial that gives you a new workout every day. The daily workout is streamed live and made available until the next episode is streamed live. This can give you a reason

59

to exercise with something new and
different each day.

- Zen Pinball- This app is a simple, old
  school game, and it is free. Who doesn't
  like pinball?

This list gives you some ideas of the types of
apps and activities you can experience by having an
Amazon Fire TV. Not only can you play music, watch
TV, and play games, but you can also use it to give you
work out sessions or storage for photos.

SOME UNIQUE APPLICATIONS OF AMAZON FIRE TV

Amazon Fire TV saw a few problems on the market, and they made some upgrades. Mainly, the production of their device was an attempt to speed up video streaming, make searching easier, and open the ability to access several different video streaming apps. However, Amazon Fire TV can change your life in more than a few ways. This chapter will describe several different surprising ways that you can use the Amazon Fire TV in your daily life.

1. **Smart Home-** Amazon Fire TV can make changes to your smart home. If you already have smart applications in your home to control different features, Alexa can change their settings for you. To use

this feature, you must have a smart home hub. This smart home hub is what will take Alexa's command from your Amazon Fire TV to the device. Some examples of compatible products are lightbulbs, air vents, thermostats, and outlets. Mostly, Alexa can turn things on and off, but with the thermostat, she can also change the temperature by a set amount of degrees. Here is one way Alexa's capability will affect your daily life. If you are sitting on the couch watching a movie and you become too cold, you can press the microphone button on your remote and change the temperature. To learn more about Alexa and Amazon echo, the author does have a detailed book about the Amazon Echo here.

2. **Watch Later-** While it has long been common that devices can record your shows and save them for later, you also have a limited amount of space. Amazon Fire TV will allow you to watch videos later, even if you didn't know when they were playing. If you don't know when they are playing, you can't save them. But with Amazon Fire TV, you can always look up channels and see what videos they have uploaded. Videos such as workout videos or religious sermons will be available to you for a set amount of time. You don't have to come at a specific time each day to catch your show. It will be available for a short time afterward.

3. **Free Workouts-** Having a variety of free workouts, even daily programs, without

having to pay could help encourage you to work out in the privacy of your home. You don't need to buy a program that you later find out is above your level, etc. You can simply go on at regular times every week and find your workouts ready for you.

4. **Learning Opportunities-** Smithsonian Earth is a specific app that you can download, and this app gives you the opportunity to learn through documentaries regularly. You do need to pay a small, monthly amount, but the amount of material you have access to is amazing. It even has 4k streaming. With so many programs intent on only entertainment, this app is great as it allows you to be entertained but learn something as well. Other apps like this

one could also provide you or your children the opportunity to learn.

5. **Connect Online-** There are many examples of apps that have a component to a regular website. Shutterfolio is an app that has been designed and connected to Shutterfly. If you often use Shutterfly, this app could help change the way you store your photos. Everyone is always running out of storage space for photos or videos, and Shutterfolio allows you extra storage space. By putting your photos in the app, you will also be able to access them from your Shutterfly account anywhere. Additionally, you can view your photos offline and upload photos quickly. If you have a lot of photos, an app like this could change your daily life.

6. **News Stories-** If you download a news app from a big news network, you will have several benefits. First, you will be able to use voice manipulation to ask Alexa about the news. She will be able to quickly pull up some of the top titles. You will also be able to follow certain news events- such as the election or a popular singer's concert route- and receive notifications when there are updates.

7. **Manage Folders-** Another unique application of the Amazon Fire TV is its ability to access and organize folders of information. If you need to read a long file but you would prefer to do so on your TV than on your phone, you can use this app to connect the devices by Bluetooth, put the folder on the TV, and read through it. You can upload, change, and

move multiple files at one time. This can also help you out with storage space if you need to save storage on your phone or tablet, but you have extra on your Amazon Fire TV box.

8. **Share Media-** One unique application Amazon Fire TV can do for you is allow all your Amazon devices to have access to the same Cloud. Let's say you have videos on your phone that you want to share with family or friends (anyone who is using your Amazon account). You can use the Amazon Cloud Drive app for your phone to put videos and photos into your Amazon's cloud, even if your phone is not an Amazon-made device. The cloud, which can be accessed by anyone on your account with internet, will then save the photos and videos. Any device logged

into your Amazon account can view the videos. This is a great way to save large videos (up to twenty minutes long) so that it does not use space but so that other family members can have access to viewing and saving them.

9. **Have a Computer-** Another unique feature about the Amazon Fire TV is that you can connect a keyboard and mouse to the Amazon Fire TV and use it like a computer. To connect them, they must have the ability to connect over Bluetooth, though some wired mouses might be compatible depending on your version of Amazon Fire TV. This can be great if you want a bigger screen to work on. It can also help you type or write anything you might need faster than clicking each letter with the remote.

10. **Low-cost Children's Material-** With an Amazon Fire TV, you will have access to a basic version of Freetime. Basically, this is a space that allows your child to play or watch programs that are safe for them. However, Amazon also offers an upgraded option. Freetime Unlimited is a feature that you will only have access to if you pay a monthly fee. If you have an Amazon Prime account, the monthly fee will be reduced. With Freetime Unlimited, material appropriate for children up to age eight would become available. This material includes appropriate movies, games, and shows. You will be able to have a free trial, then you will need to begin paying the monthly fee.

11. **Out of Country-** You can use Amazon
Fire TV in a few different countries,
meaning that if you travel to those
countries or move there, you will be able
to continue using your device. Follow
these steps to change your country:
**Manage Your Content and Devices,
Settings, Country Settings,** then
Change. You will be able to update your
country after you have entered your new
address. You should know that when you
switch countries, movies and shows that
you have purchased through Amazon
Instant Video will not be accessible to
you. Once you change back to your
original country, you will once again have
access to any purchases you made.

12. **Manage Accounts-** Because of the
smooth way that Amazon Fire TV

handles applications, you can have apps that are connected to your various accounts. This way, you can handle and manage them all your accounts with one device. Highlighting one example, MarketCast is an app that allows you to manage your stocks and bonds, watching stock prices as they rise and fall. You can watch certain stocks and receive notifications if you wish to do so. Last of all, you can keep your portfolio on the cloud that Amazon Fire TV provides so that you can long in and access your account, even if you don't have a lot of memory left on your Amazon Fire TV. This is just one of many different apps you could choose to download to manage your accounts in one place.

Amazon Fire TV has many applications that can change the way you live your daily life. As you can see, there are multiple options for the way you could choose to utilize them. I hope this chapter has given you some insight and excitement about the way you will be able to best use your Amazon Fire TV.

UNIQUE VOICE CONTROL OPTIONS OF AMAZON FIRE TV

One of the best parts about Amazon Fire TV is how well its voice program works. Many users have said that Alexa is flexible and does not need the exact command to know what you want to say. It does not exclude people with certain accents from using the voice command feature. Instead, Alexa seeks to include everyone by making it extremely easy to use her.

In this chapter, you will find an explanation of some more in-depth voice features along with some tips on using Alexa for the best results. Last of all, you will learn some answers to frequently asked questions about Alexa and some more fun questions to ask her.

Tips for Using Alexa:

Here are some tips that will help Alexa understand your voice better. If you are having trouble using her, read through these tips first and make sure that you are following the directions before you begin troubleshooting.

- Only one person should speak at a time. This is self-explanatory. What human can understand two others speaking at the same time? However, this also applies to background noise. If someone is shouting in the background, even if they are farther away from the microphone, that might cause problems for the speaker.
- Amazon recommends that you speak less than eight inches from the microphone. If you measure out eight inches with your hands, that is a large amount of space.

Additionally, make sure to give yourself at least one inch of space between you and the microphone. If you are too close or your lips are brushing up against it, then it will not be able to read your voice well.

- If you are searching for a specific movie title or singer's name, simply say the name. If you add in a bunch of extra words, then you will confuse Alexa. However, she is programmed to search for items with those key words or names.
- You can specify your searches to Prime material by adding "Prime" or "Prime only." This will mean that your search will turn back Prime material, not material that you must purchase. This is a good way to only have free results.

Frequently Asked Questions:

1. Can I use my Amazon Echo to communicate with my Amazon Fire TV? Answer: No, you need to think of the Amazon Echo and the Amazon Fire TV as two completely different devices. However, you still have many options for controlling your Amazon Fire TV. You can use your remote, the controller (if you have one), or a mobile app on your phone.

2. Will the Amazon Fire TV replace Echo's functionality? Answer: This answer depends on you. What do you use Echo for? What do you use Amazon Fire TV for? As of right now, they are still different enough that one cannot be substituted for the other. Also, by using Alexa through Amazon

Fire TV, your TV will need to be turned on to use her. Her voice will come through your television's speakers instead of a separate speaker. If you are mainly using Echo for voice commands such as setting timers or asking about the weather, then the Amazon Fire TV edition will not exclude your need for an Echo. However, you will see that Alexa adds a whole other dimension to your watching, listening, and playing experience.

3. Does Alexa improve her understanding? Answer: Yes, Alexa will adjust to your voice after a time of using her. There is an Alexa App that includes a Voice Training section. If you are having a lot of trouble with Alexa understanding you, consider downloading this app and working with it

to help her understand you better. Additionally, you can provide feedback to Amazon so they know how well she is working.

4. Can I review what I have said to Alexa?
   Answer: Yes. Once again, you must have the Alexa App to review your voice history. In **Settings**, you can click **History**, and you will be able to review interactions you have had.

5. Can I shop with Alexa?
   Answer: Alexa does enable you to shop. However, there are a few requirements and restrictions. You must have up-to-date billing information. Alexa can order music, Prime products, or other products that are in your buying history. To make this more secure, you can create a security code when making purchases so that you

do not accidentally purchase something. You can also choose to turn purchasing off if you do not wish to make any purchases with Alexa.

6. Oops, I accidentally bought something with Alexa. Can I take it back?

Answer: Yes, you can. Regular orders of non-digital products will be processed as normal if you wish to return them. Digital products can also be returned, but you must send a return and refund request before a week has passed. If more than a week has passed, you will not be eligible to return your digital product and receive a refund. As stated in question five's answer, you should set a confirmation code to prevent this from happening often.

7. Can I delete previous voice searches and recordings?

Answer: Yes, you can delete previous voice searches. You can do this by going to Amazon's website and managing your devices. However, you should know that your voice searches are saved to enhance your experience. Your favorites are kept near so that they are easily available. By deleting your voice search history, it will cause Alexa to forget your preferences and forget how she has been tuned to understand your voice.

8. Can I search through all my apps and Amazon at the same time?

Answer: No, you must either open an app (such as Netflix) and search it manually, or you must search through Amazon video only. There is not a way, even though voice searching, that you can access both at the same time.

9. Can I use voice searching to start playing a show's season in the middle?

   Answer: No, voice searching is set up to access the next episode in the series you name. If you last watched episode eight of season two, then episode nine will instantly start playing once you have searched the name. If you have never watched a series before, then playing the show through voice search will cause it to start from episode one of season one. Right now, there is not an option to start on episode three, for example, even if you have never watched the series before. You will manually need to skip to the episode.

10. How can Alexa control my music?

Answer: Alexa has a lot of features and will be able to help you in many ways; however, there are some limitations. You can use some basic commands such as "Pause," "Stop," "Restart," or "Skip Song," but you cannot fast forward to a certain part of the song using Alexa. Additionally, the music app is separate from the music you can stream straight from Amazon, and Alexa will not have access to commands within an app.

Alexa's Easter Eggs

One of the fun ways to play around with the voice commands are by asking a list of fun questions. This feature is part of what makes Amazon Fire TV's voice mechanism so unique. Part of the entertainment value is that there are several answers for each question, so you might try asking them more than once. Here are a few more of these questions, as this is by no means a complete list. Enjoy the fun you will have with Alexa.

- Execute order 66.
- Romeo, Romeo, wherefore art thou Romeo?
- What is the meaning of life?
- Is there a Santa?
- Do you have a boyfriend?
- What is your favorite color?
- Do aliens exist?
- Where do you live?
- How much wood would a wood chuck chuck if a wood chuck could chuck wood?
- Who let the dogs out?
- What color are your eyes?
- How do you spell supercalifragilisticexpialidocious?

- Who's on first?
- Who is the fairest of them all?
- What do you think of Google?
- What do you think of Apple?
- Do you know the Muffin Man?
- Do you know the way to San Jose?
- What's in a name?
- When am I going to die?
- Do you know Siri? Are you better than Siri?
- Where was George Washington buried?
- Where are my keys?
- How much do you weigh?
- Are you lying?

There are quite a few more that are also fun. If you are interested in a complete list, google "Alexa's Easter Eggs," and you will find hundreds of fun questions to ask her.

Operating the voice feature in Amazon Fire TV is not difficult. Often if you have problems with the remote being recognized, simply restarting the Amazon Fire TV box will reset the problem. The best part of the voice control is that Alexa learns from you. Your voice recordings are saved, and Alexa learns to adjust to your accent or your way of saying things even more. Your experience with Amazon Fire TV is guaranteed to have one of the easiest searching mechanisms and experiences overall because of voice control.

CONCLUSION

In the end, you will find yourself pleased with your decision to purchase Amazon Fire TV. Its versatile design means that it can serve as many different gadgets for you. You can use it to store game memory or photos, movies or music. The remote and the voice searching mean that you will experience high, fast performance.

Another bonus feature that makes the Amazon Fire TV a great addition to your home is its impressive list of apps compatible with it. You will be able to watch any show or movie and can play any of the popular games, without needing another device.

Amazon Fire TV is relatively easy for new users to understand and begin working. Some people have trouble understanding technology, but the lack of cluttered buttons on the remote means that it will be easy to explain how to use it. Besides, if you do not understand how to locate or find some feature, the device's voice search feature will give you some help.

Amazon Fire TV is worth the money to purchase it and find space around your TV for this streaming device. It will change the way you stream media, and it will also make your day just a little bit more fun with Alexa's interesting answers to your questions.

I hope you enjoy using your Amazon Fire TV, and I hope I have answered your questions and given you a great user experience.

60478341R00052

Made in the USA
Middletown, DE
30 December 2017